Surviving Floods

Elizabeth Raum

Chicago, Illinois

www.heinemannraintree.com
Visit our website to find out
more information about
Heinemann-Raintree books.

To order:
☎ Phone 888-454-2279
💻 Visit www.heinemannraintree.com
to browse our catalog and order online.

Edited by Louise Galpine and Laura Knowles
Designed by Victoria Allen
Original illustrations © Capstone Global Library
    Limited 2011
Illustrated by HLSTUDIOS
Picture research by Ruth Blair

Originated by Capstone Global Library Limited
Printed and bound in China by CTPS

15 14 13 12 11
10 9 8 7 6 5 4 3 2 1

Library of Congress Cataloging-in-Publication Data
Raum, Elizabeth.
  Surviving floods / Elizabeth Raum.
    p. cm.—(Children's true stories : natural disaster)
  Includes bibliographical references and index.
  ISBN 978-1-4109-4091-9—ISBN 978-1-4109-4098-8 (pbk.)
  1. Floods—Juvenile literature. 2. Emergency management—
Juvenile literature. I. Title.
  GB1399.R38 2012
  363.34'93—dc22   2010036181

Acknowledgments
We would like to thank the following for permission to
reproduce photographs: © Corbis pp. **8**, 11; Corbis pp. **5**
(© HO/Reuters), **17** (© Brooks Kraft/Sygma), **18** (© Andrew
Holbrooke), **19** (© Andrew Holbrooke), **23** (© Gideon Mendel
for Action Aid), **24** (© RAFIQUR RAHMAN/Reuters), **26**
(© STRINGER/epa); Getty Images pp. **4** (Carsten Koall),
14 (Topical Press Agency), **20** (Chris Wilkins/AFP), **21** (Joe
Raedle); © Glenn Baker, Easy Like Water p. **25**; © Johnstown
Area Heritage Association Archives p. **7**; Library of Congress
p. **9** (George Barker); Superstock pp. **13** (© Science and
Society), **15** (© The Francis Frith Collection).

Cover photograph of a girl carrying her sister on her shoulder
wading through a water logged road through a suburb in
Dhaka, Bangladesh, 19 September 2004 reproduced with
permission of Corbis/© Rafiqur Rahman/Reuters.

Quotations on pages 7, 9, and 10 are from David G.
McCullogh, *The Johnstown Flood* (New York: Simon &
Schuster, 1987). Quotation on page 8 is from Christine Gibson,
"Our 10 Greatest Natural Disasters," *American Heritage
Magazine*, August/September 2006, vol. 57, issue 4. Mosa
Rita's story on page 23 is from Helen Rowe, "Hope Floats for
Bangladeshi Children on School Boats," October 8, 2007,
The Brunei Times.

The author would like to thank Richard Lord, Lindsey
Pieper, and Mohammed Rezwan for so generously sharing
their stories.

We would like to thank Daniel Block for his invaluable help
in the preparation of this book.

Every effort has been made to contact copyright holders
of material reproduced in this book. Any omissions will
be rectified in subsequent printings if notice is given to
the publisher.

Disclaimer
All the Internet addresses (URLs) given in this book were valid
at the time of going to press. However, due to the dynamic
nature of the Internet, some addresses may have changed, or
sites may have changed or ceased to exist since publication.
While the author and publisher regret any inconvenience this
may cause readers, no responsibility for any such changes can
be accepted by either the author or the publisher.

Contents

DAILY LIFE
Read here to learn about what life was like for the children in these stories, and the impact the disaster had at home and school.

NUMBER CRUNCHING
Find out here the details about natural disasters and the damage they cause.

Survivors' lives
Read these boxes to find out what happened to the children in this book when they grew up.

HELPING HAND
Find out how people and organizations have helped to save lives.

On the scene
Read eyewitness accounts of the natural disasters in the survivors' own words.

Some words are printed in bold, **like this**. You can find out what they mean by looking in the glossary on page 30.

Introduction

A flood is when water covers land that is normally dry. When too much rain soaks an area, it causes rivers to rise, and water pours out over land. Melting snow, high **tides**, hurricanes, and seasonal rains—such as Asia's **monsoon rains**—may cause floods. Some areas, called **flood plains**, flood every few years. Sometimes floods occur in areas that have been dry for 100 years or more.

Melting snow caused flooding in the town of Koenigstein, Germany, in April 2006.

DAILY LIFE

Floods affect thousands of children every year. Some barely escape with their lives. Others watch as floodwater damages their homes and schools. Floods, like other natural disasters, can change lives forever.

NUMBER CRUNCHING

It takes only about 15 centimeters (6 inches) of fast-moving water to knock a person down. A car begins to float in 60 centimeters (2 feet) of water.

Flash floods

Some floods happen slowly, trapping towns or villages as the water rises around them. **Flash floods** happen quickly, often without warning. Too much rain, melting snow, broken **dykes** or **dams**, high tides, or hurricanes can cause flash floods. People may be trapped in homes or cars by the rising water. Fast-moving water may float houses off their foundations or sweep cars into deep water.

The Cumberland River flooded areas of Tennessee in May 2010, leaving 22 people dead and forcing thousands to leave their homes.

Johnstown, Pennsylvania: 1889

In Johnstown, Pennsylvania, May 30, 1889, was Memorial Day. People had the day off and went shopping or watched a parade. By the middle of the afternoon, it began to rain. More than 25 centimeters (10 inches) of rain fell on the nearby mountains. Rivers and lakes swelled.

Six-year-old Gertrude Quinn saw worry in her father's face. The South Fork Dam, built in 1852, was only 22 kilometers (14 miles) away from the town. If the **dam** were to burst, water would pour into Johnstown.

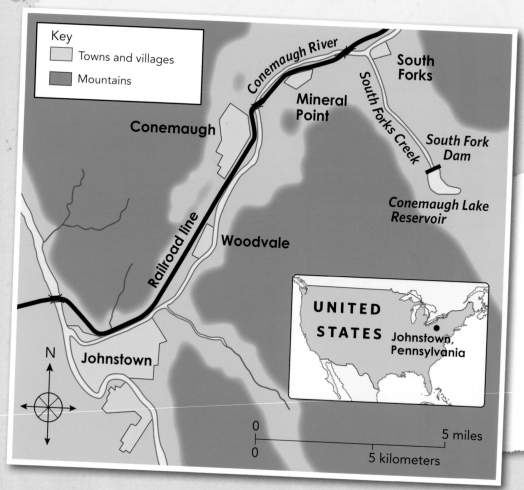

Key
- Towns and villages
- Mountains

Conemaugh River
South Forks
Mineral Point
South Forks Creek
Conemaugh
South Fork Dam
Conemaugh Lake Reservoir
Railroad line
Woodvale
Johnstown

UNITED STATES
Johnstown, Pennsylvania

N

| 0 | 5 miles |
| 0 | 5 kilometers |

This map shows the Johnstown area. When the South Fork Dam burst, floodwaters flowed down the Conemaugh River toward Johnstown.

DAILY LIFE

In 1889 there were no telephones, radios, or cars in Johnstown. Messages were delivered by hand. Many children spent the rainy day before the flood reading, doing chores, or playing board games.

Run!

The next morning, Mr. Quinn ordered Gertrude to stay inside. But Gertrude disobeyed him. She sat on the porch and dipped her feet into the rainwater. Ducks swam by. Just before 4:00 p.m., her father came home from work. As he was scolding Gertrude, he heard a rushing noise.

Mr. Quinn saw a wall of water rushing toward Johnstown. "Run for your lives," he shouted. The dam had burst.

This photo of Gertrude was taken before the Johnstown flood.

Disaster

Gertrude's father carried one of Gertrude's sisters. Her other sister was big enough to walk through the water. Libby Hipp, their 18-year-old nanny, carried Gertrude. Gertrude's Aunt Abbie, who was visiting, carried her own baby. But as the water rose higher and higher, Aunt Abbie was afraid. She turned back. So did Libby.

After the flood, people looked through the damaged buildings, trying to find anything of value.

On the scene

Sixteen-year-old Victor Heiser was in Johnstown on the day of the flood. He later wrote, "I could see a huge wall advancing with incredible **rapidity** down the diagonal street. It was not recognizable as water, it was a dark mass [with] **seethed** houses, **freight cars**, trees, and animals."

Separated

Gertrude kicked and screamed, calling, "Papa, Papa!" But it was too late. Her father was on the hill, and Gertrude was back at the house with Libby and Aunt Abbie. As Mr. Quinn watched from the hillside, the house —with Gertrude inside—rocked back and forth, tipped over, and disappeared into the rushing waters.

The flood destroyed hundreds of homes and left about 25,000 people homeless.

NUMBER CRUNCHING

Around 2,200 people died in the flood. That was 1 out of every 10 people who lived in Johnstown.

Swept away

When the house tipped into the river, Gertrude fell onto a muddy mattress that was floating in the water. She yelled for help. A mill worker named Maxwell McArchren jumped from a nearby rooftop onto the mattress. Another man, in the window of a nearby house, called, "Throw that baby over here!"

McArchren tossed Gertrude 3 to 4.5 meters (10 to 15 feet) across the water. Luckily, someone caught her! Gertrude was so frightened that she did not say a word until her father found her the next day. Gertrude was lucky. Many others died, including Libby Hipp, Aunt Abbie, and her baby.

HELPING HAND

The Johnstown flood was the first major disaster dealt with by the American Red Cross. Clara Barton, who founded the Red Cross in 1881, spent five months in Johnstown setting up hospitals, kitchens, and emergency housing. People from across the United States and 14 other countries sent money and supplies.

Rebuilding

After the waters **receded**, Mr. Quinn sent Gertrude to stay with relatives in Pittsburgh, about 120 kilometers (75 miles) away. Many others left, too. However, like Gertrude, they returned when homes and schools were rebuilt. The survivors never forgot the Johnstown flood. It changed their lives forever.

After the flood, people lived in caves, tents, or huts built of scraps until they could rebuild their houses.

United Kingdom: 1953

Saturday, January 31, 1953, was a cold, clear night in towns along the coast of the North Sea. The North Sea lies between the United Kingdom and northwest Europe. People enjoyed their usual activities. They had no idea that a gigantic flood was on the way.

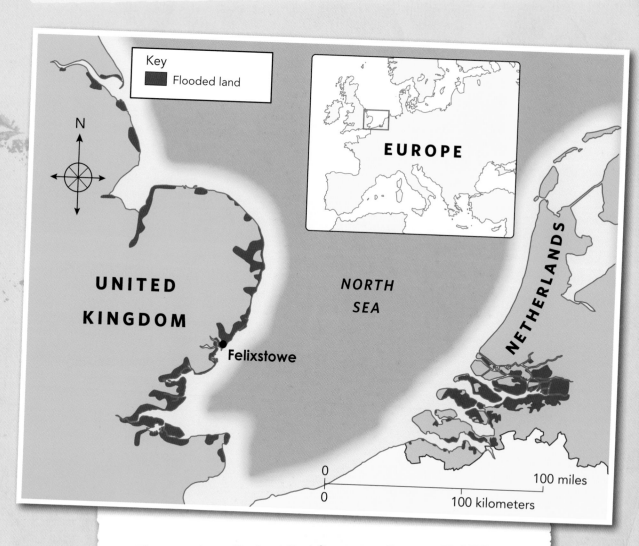

Key
Flooded land

EUROPE

UNITED KINGDOM

NORTH SEA

NETHERLANDS

Felixstowe

0
0
100 miles
100 kilometers

This map shows the land that flooded on January 31, 1953. Strong winds sent seawater into towns and cities along both North Sea coasts.

Richard's story

Seven-year-old Richard Lord lived in the seaside town of Felixstowe, England (see map). That evening, Richard and his parents went to a movie. They stopped for dinner on the way home, and then Richard went to bed.

Around midnight, Richard's parents rushed into his room. They woke him up. The water in his room was already waist deep. Richard was scared. He could not swim.

Richard's father lifted him onto the roof. Both parents joined him. They spent the night huddled on the roof, as water rose around them.

This photo, taken from the air, shows how the flooding turned streets and fields into lakes.

On the scene

Richard remembers the night of the flood: "We lay on the roof, my parents on either side of me to keep me warm. Although I was frightened, I remember seeing everything happening. It was still clear and bright, but a very strong wind blew through the night. It was very, very cold."

Rescuers used rowboats to check houses and take people to safety.

Rescue

Throughout the night, Richard heard neighbors scream, and he saw trees, pieces of houses, and even a cow float past. Floodwaters lifted the house off its foundations and carried it away for several streets.

The next morning, rescuers in rowboats carried Richard and his family to dry land. Richard did not learn until later that several of his friends had not survived.

HELPING HAND

Richard believes his parents saved his life that night. He said: "I lay between them both to keep warm from their body heat. Without them, I would have died."

Preventing more disasters

Strong winds sent water from the North Sea pouring into towns along the English coast. The same storm also caused death and destruction in the Netherlands.

After the 1953 flood, both England and the Netherlands built barriers made of concrete and steel along the coasts. In England, **engineers** rebuilt beaches of sand or loose rocks in front of these **seawalls**. The beaches break the force of the waves. This protects the seawalls, which then hold back the water.

On Canvey Island, England, a sandy beach in front of a seawall helps to prevent flooding.

NUMBER CRUNCHING

This chart shows how many people died and how much damage was caused by the North Sea floods.

	Eastern England	The Netherlands
Deaths	307	1,835
Houses damaged	around 24,000	around 46,000
Land flooded	728 square kilometers (281 square miles)	1,305 square kilometers (504 square miles)

Mississippi River: 1993

The Mississippi River has been flooding for thousands of years. As melting snow and summer rains swell the river, it flows into the nearby **wetlands**. The wetlands act like sponges, soaking up the extra water.

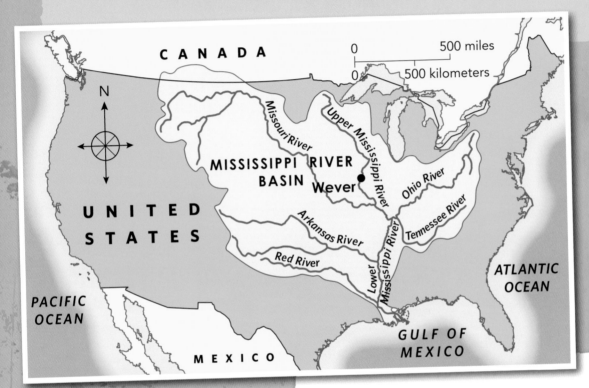

Several major rivers drain into the Mississippi River, leading to flooding during the spring and summer.

Record rains

When people began settling along the Mississippi River, they turned the wetlands into farms, towns, and cities. To protect against flooding, they built **levees** to hold the river back. These usually worked. But in 1993, record amounts of rain fell. Nothing could hold back the Mighty Mississippi or the 150 rivers and **tributaries** that join with the Mississippi, forming the world's third-largest **river basin**.

HELPING HAND

When the Mississippi River began to burst through its levees and threatened to overflow, whole communities joined together to build sandbag **dykes** to hold the water back. Thousands of people filled bags with sand and stacked them up to form dykes. Older children helped fill sandbags. Younger children delivered food and drinks to the volunteers.

These volunteers are building sandbag dykes near Des Moines, Iowa.

NUMBER CRUNCHING

Rivers involved	150
Days flood lasted	200 days in some locations
States involved	9
Total land area involved	1,036,000 square kilometers (400,000 square miles)
Farmlands flooded	60,700 square kilometers (23,440 square miles)
Failed levees	1,000
Towns completely flooded	75
Homes destroyed	10,000
Deaths	50

Lindsey's story

In 1993, eight-year-old Lindsey Pieper lived on a large farm in Wever, Iowa (see map on page 16). There were 35 kilometers (22 miles) of levees surrounding the farm to protect it from the river, which was 3.2 kilometers (2 miles) away. If the levees broke, the farm would flood.

When the levees broke, the Mississippi River overflowed its banks and flooded nearby farms and towns.

Preparing for disaster

In July, Lindsey's dad told everyone to prepare for a flood. Lindsey was worried. What did he mean?

The family packed clothing and supplies. Friends came to help move heavy furniture to the second floor of the farmhouse, and volunteers worked day and night to repair and rebuild failing levees. Lindsey carried food and drinks to them.

Despite their efforts, the levees leaked. The day before they broke, Lindsey's family moved. They stayed in a crowded hotel room for two weeks. Lindsey was safe and dry, but she worried about the future.

The Mississippi River flowed into farm fields and buildings.

HELPING HAND

Lindsey's parents spent time explaining the situation to their children. "If we had questions or were scared, they made us feel comfortable," Lindsey says. Most importantly, they made sure the children were safe both before and after the farm flooded.

The mess

After the waters began to **recede**, Lindsey and her family returned to the farm by boat. "The house smelled awful," Lindsey remembers. The first floor walls were wet and crumbling, and dead fish lay on the floor.

This photo shows a U.S. Coast Guard boat traveling though the city center of a town in Iowa that was also flooded by the Mississippi River.

HELPING HAND

Many volunteer groups helped to rebuild the Piepers' home. Whenever she sits on the front porch, Lindsey remembers the church group that rebuilt it. Laura, a teenage volunteer, took time to play and joke with Lindsey.

The clean-up operation

Cleaning up after a flood was a big job. Many houses and buildings had to be taken down. Schools and hospitals were damaged. So were 10 airports. Trains and river barges stopped moving for several weeks.

In many homes, the entire first floor, including furniture, flooring, and walls, was destroyed.

Lindsey's life now

Lindsey's family still lives on the farm in Wever, Iowa. In 2008 the Mississippi River flooded again. Lindsey, who is now a college student, was in charge of supplying food and drinks to volunteer flood fighters. Her entire family wanted to help others as they had been helped in 1993.

Bangladesh: 2007

In 2007, **monsoon rains** flooded many areas of Bangladesh. In some areas, floods occur yearly. In the hilly areas of northeastern Bangladesh, rivers overflow each spring and fall. Melting **glaciers** in the Himalayan Mountains send floodwaters into the valleys.

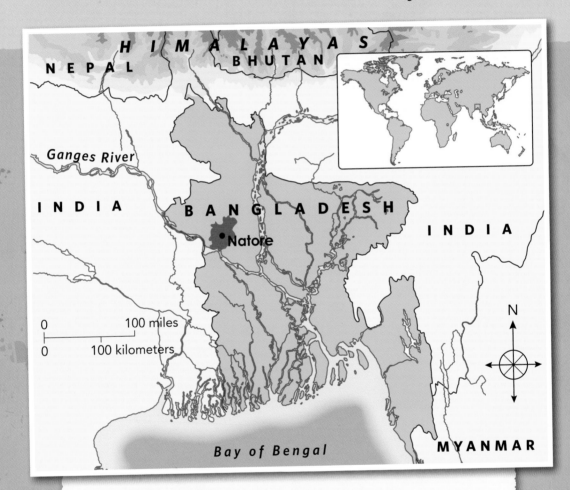

Most of Bangladesh is very flat, with many rivers. Every year, the Ganges River and other major rivers carry melting snow from the Himalayan Mountains into towns and villages.

NUMBER CRUNCHING

In Bangladesh in 2007, two major floods destroyed 337 schools and damaged around 5,000 others.

Mosa's story

Mosa Rita, who was seven years old in 2007, spent her days as a housemaid. She cleaned and cooked for another family in her village in the Natore district of Bangladesh (see map). Her father was a fisherman. Her family relied on the money that Mosa earned as a maid.

Hard work has always been part of Mosa's life. So are floods. But it is not easy. Schools close for about four months of each year due to floods.

Happily for Mosa Rita, architect Mohammed Rezwan has a solution: floating schools.

These children, who lost their homes in the 2007 flood, are lining up for a bowl of rice.

23

Floating schools

During the 2007 floods, Mosa Rita went to school on a boat. Every evening at 6:30 p.m., the school boat picked her up on the riverbank. She left school at 9:00 p.m. "The teachers teach us very well," she said. Education makes her future brighter.

Getting to school during floods is difficult because the streets are filled with floodwater.

Mohammed Rezwan

When Mohammed Rezwan was a boy, **seasonal floods** closed his school. The problem of closed schools always bothered him. In 2002 he developed a solution. He designed boats as classrooms. These boats are fitted with multilayered waterproof roofs. The boats use **solar power** to run lights and computers. Solar lights allow students to study after dark. Rezwan plans to add more floating schools, libraries, and even hospitals.

"I believe that if children cannot come to school then the school should go to them," Rezwan has said. He has received many awards for his great idea.

Floating schools allow children to attend school even during floods.

On the scene

"When we attend the boat school, we enjoy ourselves," a nine-year-old girl named Shakila Khatoon said in Bengali, the national language. "It's different from other schools."

Conclusion

It is impossible to prevent all floods. Rain, melting snow, and high **tides** are part of nature. But **engineers** have worked hard to protect cities and towns from repeated flooding. **Levees** and other barriers help to keep rivers under control. **Dams** are checked regularly, so they are less likely to burst. **Seawalls**, like the ones in eastern England and in the Netherlands, protect coastal towns and villages.

Tropical storms led to severe flooding in the Australian states of Queensland and Victoria in December 2010 and January 2011. Huge areas of land were flooded, affecting around 200,000 people.

HELPING HAND

Today, weather satellites help forecasters predict floods before they happen. Flood warnings appear on television, radio, and the Internet. If people know a flood is expected, they can move to safety before the waters reach them.

Climate change

The floods in Bangladesh are made worse by our changing climate. As Earth gets warmer, **glaciers** like the ones high in the Himalayas melt. This sends more water into the already high rivers. **Global warming** also causes the sea to rise. This floods low-lying coastal areas.

Saving forests and wetlands

Floods also become more likely when forests are cut down. Forests prevent floods in several ways. Tree roots absorb water, and leaves protect the soil from heavy rains. This prevents erosion (washing away of the soil). Saving forests helps to prevent floods.

Wetlands act as "sponges" during floods, preventing floodwaters from spreading so far or fast. Most dams and **dykes** stop rivers from spreading out to the wetlands. This means that when floods occur, they may be even more **severe**. Today, engineers are building better types of dams and dykes that protect wetlands and forests, as well as people. In the future, these new kinds of dams will help prevent damage from major floods.

Mapping Floods

Floods can occur anywhere at anytime, especially after heavy rains. People living along seacoasts and major rivers are most likely to experience flooding.

NORTH AMERICA

Mississippi Drainage Basin

•Johnstown, Pennsylvania

ATLANTIC OCEAN

PACIFIC OCEAN

SOUTH AMERICA

Johnstown, Pennsylvania

Flash floods, like the one that destroyed Johnstown, Pennsylvania, in 1889, may occur when a dam or levee breaks. Today, dams are checked often and repaired when necessary.

Mississippi River

When the Mississippi River overflowed in 1993, floodwaters destroyed thousands of homes and businesses. Restoring wetlands along rivers and coastlines helps prevent seasonal flooding.

England and the Netherlands

In 1953 heavy rains and high waves flooded coastal towns in England and the Netherlands. Hurricanes and tropical storms are a constant threat in coastal areas.

ENGLAND

Felixstowe   NETHERLANDS

EUROPE

ASIA

AFRICA

BANGLADESH

Natore

PACIFIC OCEAN

INDIAN OCEAN

AUSTRALIA

Bangladesh

Flooding in Bangladesh is increasing as Earth's climate changes. Small children, old people, and the poor are most likely to die during natural disasters such as floods or hurricanes.

ANTARCTICA

Glossary

dam body of water held in by a barrier

dyke bank built to control or hold back the water of a sea or a river

engineer person who constructs or manages building projects

flash flood flood that happens quickly, often without warning, usually caused by heavy rain, melting snow, high tides, or hurricanes

flood plain nearly flat plain along the course of a stream or river that is naturally likely to flood

freight car train car designed to carry cargo

glacier huge mass of ice formed by compacted snow that slowly flows over a landmass

global warming gradual rising of Earth's temperature

levee dyke formed from earth, designed to prevent the flooding of a river

monsoon rain rains that fall during the rainy season in Bangladesh, India, and nearby lands

rapidity extreme quickness

recede go away or withdraw

river basin land area that is drained by a river and the streams that flow into it

seasonal flood flood that happens around the same time every year

seawall strong wall designed to prevent flooding from the sea

seethe surge or foam as if boiling

severe extremely bad

solar power energy from the sun

tide rise and fall of the sea level on the shore

tributary stream that flows to a larger stream or other body of water

wetland land that has a wet and spongy soil, such as a marsh, swamp, or bog

Find Out More

Books

Chambers, Catherine. *Flood* (*Wild Weather*). Chicago: Heinemann Library, 2007.

Jeffrey, Gary. *Tsunamis and Floods* (*Graphic Natural Disasters*). New York: Rosen, 2007.

Spilsbury, Louise, and Richard Spilsbury. *Raging Floods* (*Awesome Forces of Nature*). Chicago: Heinemann Library, 2010.

Websites

www.fema.gov/kids/floods.htm
This U.S. government website tells what to do in the event of a flood.

www.pbs.org/wgbh/nova/flood/
This PBS website offers a variety of features about floods, including video footage of the 1993 flood that hit parts of the midwestern United States.

www.weatherwizkids.com/weather-rain.htm
The Weather WizKids website has flood information, plus all kinds of other weather facts.

www.worldweather.org
The World Meteorological Organization website gives official weather observations and forecasts from all around the world.

Index